Breaking the Spirit of Addiction

Breaking the Spirit of Addiction

Biblical principles to release the human spirit from the bondage of Addiction

Randy Hunter

To order additional copies of this book, contact:
Xlibris Corporation
1-888-795-4274
www.Xlibris.com
Orders@Xlibris.com

41638

Contents

THIS BOOK IS DEDICATED TO ALL THOSE PEOPLE WHO HAVE
LOST FAMILY AND CLOSE FRIENDS TO THE SPIRITUAL
BONDAGE OF DRUG ADDICTION. IT IS MY HOPE THAT
GOD WILL USE THIS BOOK AS A VESSEL FOR HIS WORD.
IT IS MY PRAYER THAT ALL THOSE THAT HAVE LOST LOVED ONES
WILL GAIN COMFORT, INSPIRATION AND HOPE THAT NO
ONE ELSE HAS TO DIE FROM THE BONDAGE
OF DRUG ADDICTION.
AND FINALLY, I PRAY THAT GOD WILL GET THE HONOR
AND GLORY FOR THOSE THAT ARE SAVED FROM DEATH'S DOOR
THROUGH THE KNOWLEDGE GAINED IN THIS BOOK.

Foreword

The epidemic of drug addiction has ruined untold countless lives in the United States and throughout the entire world. As events in the world seem to become progressively worse, so does the problem of drug addiction. I have personally fought the war on drugs, having a career in narcotics law enforcement. Even though God has blessed me to have great success in my career as a narcotics officer, I have come to understand that the only way to rid society of narcotics abuse is to stop the demand. The old business adage of "supply and demand" runs especially true in the narcotics "industry". If people in society want illicit drugs of abuse, someone somewhere is going to produce, grow, manufacture, transport and sell them. I believe that God has called me to minister to anyone that will listen about how to get our families and friends freed from the bondage of drug addiction that is destroying this generation.

I have been asked many times by many people about what they could do to help their family and friends that are under the influence of drug abuse. At the time, I didn't have many answers to give them. I then began to ask God in prayer to help me understand the problem of addiction and what God's Word said about it. God answered my prayer and began to give me revelation on this topic. I was inspired by God to primarily focus on the source of drug addiction and how to defeat it. This book was written as a way to learn and understand what God's Holy Word, The Bible, says about addictions. It was meant to be used as a handbook on how you can change lives of others.

In writing this book, I want to advise and challenge all those who will read this prelude, that this book is totally based on the Word of God, and faith in the Word, and that Our Heavenly Father is true to keep His word and promises. It is my hope and prayer that you do not just read this book and reference scriptures in it. You need to sit down with your Bible as you read through this book and do your own study and research about these scriptures, it is only then will the Word totally come alive and allow you to receive full revelation about this. It is my opinion that no one should ever completely take someone's word for what the Bible says; you need to know what it says for yourself. You see, the Bible can be very intimidating to read due to its sheer size and many books. Some of it may even be hard to understand. This book is meant to be a guide on the spiritual root of addiction and how to combat it. Its purpose is to enhance a Bible study so you can have guidance and enlightenment on this subject and then you can walk away with a true and real understanding. This book is meant to guide you, encourage you, enlighten you and assist you in your understanding of the Word on the topic of the roots of addiction and the principles involved in dealing with it.

As you are reading this, there is someone in either your family or a friend that comes to mind that you are concerned about their addiction to illicit drugs. I ask that you give this book ten minutes of your time and read through the first chapter about the source of addictions. After that, it is my prayer that the word of God will take root in your heart to grow and that you understand that you do not have to sit idly by and watch friends and loved ones destroyed by addiction, but that you can learn how to break the spirit of addiction.

Introduction

Everyone knows that our country is involved in a war today. We all have friends and family that are being affected because of this war. There is fighting in the streets and American men and women are dying as casualties of this war every day. It is talked about in the news headlines everyday. People are talking about it, sometimes even choosing sides. Our politicians are using it as a political campaign issue. This war is right in our own backyard. It is a war on the spiritual force of addiction.

Over the years I have witnessed people destroy their lives by becoming hooked on illicit drugs. These people have been from all walks of life, wealthy people, famous people, movie stars, political figures, school teachers, police officers, people from the elderly population, young children, you name it, and there have been people from that segment of the population that have been affected by illicit drugs.

There is nothing that affects me more than seeing the eyes of children in a residence, where their family is using, selling or manufacturing drugs. You can see the despair in their eyes. These children have been witnesses to things that we do not even want to imagine. All the while, I am reminded that these children should not have to live in these conditions, they should be enjoying their childhood, but far too often, they are the ones that take the brunt of the effects that drug addiction has on their families.

What are we to do? As a Christian, I have learned through the wisdom of God that we have the authority to take control of these situations, through the Word of God, and save our families and friends from dying at the hand of this plague. It's at this point you are probably asking how. It is God's purpose for me to write this book and instruct you and to help build your faith in God's word, so that you will know exactly what to do, how to do it, when to do it and to expect results from it.

The book of Revelation speaks about drug abuse as being one of the plagues during the times of tribulation, let us take a look;

Rev 9:17-10:1

17 And thus I saw the horses in the vision, and them that sat on them, having breastplates of fire, and of jacinth, and brimstone: and the heads of the horses were as the heads of lions; and out of their mouths issued fire and smoke and brimstone.
18 By these three was the third part of men killed, by the fire, and by the smoke, and by the brimstone, which issued out of their mouths.
19 For their power is in their mouth, and in their tails: for their tails were like unto serpents, and had heads, and with them they do hurt.
20 And the rest of the men which were not killed by these plagues yet **repented not** of the works of their hands, that they should not worship devils, and idols of gold, and silver, and brass, and stone, and of wood: which neither can see, nor hear, nor walk:
21 **Neither repented they** of their murders, nor of their **sorceries**, nor of their fornication, nor of their thefts.
KJV

We can see here that there will come a time in the near future that people will not repent of their sorceries. If you look up the actual Greek word (Greek was the original language of the New Testament writings) for sorceries that is used here, you will find that it is a derivative of the word "pharmakeia". The definition of pharmakeia is medication, and this is where we get the words, pharmacy, pharmacist and pharmaceuticals. According to several biblical resources, when sorcerers of biblical times, conducted their "magic", they often utilized potions or concoctions. Now, before you get confused, I am not condemning today's advancements of medicine. God has blessed us with tremendous advances, knowledge and wisdom in this area. The point that I am trying to make here is what is in the Word. The Word tells us that there will come a time that men will not repent of there sorceries (medication abuses). We are not at this point in time, yet. There is still hope and through key points in this book we can help our friends and loved ones out of this bondage.

This book is for those that are at their wits-end with family members and it appears that all hope is lost. For those which are willing to take a chance that God's Word is true and faithful. If you are willing to not let the outside world affect you and are ready to let God lead you and ready to see lives changed and a miracle performed, buckle up because we are going to take a journey, we are now on a mission for God.

1

The Spiritual Root of Addiction

Society often wonders why serial killers, murderers, rapists and other unthinkable types of criminals do what they do. Here are some of their questions. Why do people walk on to school campuses and shed innocent blood of family and friends? How could people do unspeakable things to children that are placed in their care, mentally scarring them for life? How and why would God allow these things to happen? Millions of dollars are spent trying to understand and reason what is their motivation. They are evaluated as to whether they are competent to stand trial and often times the "yardstick" used to measure their competency is flawed. These people ***do not think*** as normal people in society do and are not always understood.

The Bible teaches about principalities, powers and spiritual wickedness in high places. It is these spiritual forces that are the reason that some people do the unspeakable things that they do. That little voice inside of you that says, "Go ahead it will be okay", or "no one will ever know". It is this influence from Satan and his angels that get people into trouble. I know that you may already be saying, I am not so sure what this guy is talking about, but let's take a look at what the Bible says about these matters before you close this book and forget all about finishing it. First of all, the Bible says in Revelation Chapter 12:7-9

7   And there was war in heaven: Michael and His angels fought against the dragon; and the dragon fought and his angels,
8   And prevailed not; neither was their place found any more in heaven.

9   And the great dragon *was cast out*, that old serpent, called the Devil, and Satan, which deceiveth the whole world: *he was cast out* into the earth, and *his angels were cast out with Him*.
KJV

So, here we find out that when Satan rebelled in Heaven against God, Satan and his angels (those angels that believed and followed Satan) were cast down to earth. Now let us look at Ephesians chapter 6 and see what Paul was trying to tell us about these forces. Ephesians 6:11-12 says

11 Put on the whole armour of God, that ye may be able to *stand against the wiles of the devil*.
12 For we wrestle *not against flesh and blood*, but against *principalities*, against *powers*, against the *rulers of the darkness* of this world, against *spiritual wickedness* in high places.
KJV

What Paul says here is the problem is not with people, it is with the *forces of evil* in this earth that drive them to do what it is that they do. People can and do become influenced by forces that they *DO NOT* understand. That, my dear friend is how Satan works. He *lies*, *deceives*, *tricks*, *manipulates, twists* and what ever else he can do to get you to do what he wants. He will give reasons of justification for what he wants people to do. That is how he gets control over them. Look at what is said in 2 Timothy 2:22-26

22 Flee also *youthful lusts*: but follow righteousness, faith, charity, peace, with them that call on the Lord out of a pure heart.
23 But foolish and unlearned questions avoid, knowing that they do gender strifes.
24 And the servant of the Lord must not strive; but be gentle unto all men, apt to teach, patient,
25 In meekness instructing those that oppose themselves; if God peradventure will give them repentance to the acknowledging of the truth;
26 And that they may recover themselves *out of the snare of the devil, who are taken captive by him at his will*.
KJV

The problem that people have is that if they do not have a true relationship with their savior, Jesus, and God, the Heavenly father, they can easily become tricked into one of Satan's lies, snares and traps.
Let us look at what the Word says how Satan gets people into this position.

2 Corinthians 4:3-6

3   But if our gospel be hid, *it is hid to them that are lost:*
4   In whom the god of this world *hath blinded the minds of them which believe not*, *lest the light* of the glorious gospel *of Christ*, who is the image of God, *should shine unto them*.
5   For we preach not ourselves, but Christ Jesus the Lord; and ourselves your servants for Jesus' sake.
6   For God, who commanded the light to shine out of darkness, hath shined in our hearts, to *give the light of the knowledge of the glory of God in the face of Jesus Christ*.
KJV

The "god of this world" has the mind of unbelievers blinded. Who is the "god of this world" that is being referred to in verse 4; it is Satan or the Devil. What we have to do is go before our Heavenly Father, through Jesus our savior and ask that the person or loved one that we are standing for have the blind removed from their eyes, so that "the light of the knowledge of the glory of God" can be shown to them.

Look at what is said in John 8:42-44

42 Jesus said unto them, If God were your Father, ye would love me: for I proceeded forth and came from God; neither came I of myself, but he sent me.
43 Why do ye not understand my speech? *even because ye cannot hear my word.*
44 Ye are of your father the devil, *and the lusts of your father ye will do*. He was a *murderer* from the beginning, and abode not in the truth, because there is *no truth in him*. When he speaketh a lie, he speaketh of his own: for he is a *liar*, and the father of it. KJV

What Jesus was telling these folks is that they were blinded by Satan and he had taken them captive to do his will that is why in verse 43 Jesus told them that they could not understand what he was trying to tell them. Then He goes on to call Satan a *murderer* and a *liar*. John 10:10 puts it this way;

10 The thief cometh not, but for to *steal*, and to *kill*, and to *destroy*: *I am come that they might have **life,** and that they might have it more **abundantly**.*
KJV

Jesus again called Satan a thief that comes only to kill, steal and destroy. Satan is doing this very work today through the evils of drug abuse and addiction by stealing the joy from families, killing our loved ones and destroying the hope of millions through the bondage of drug addiction. But at the end of verse 10 there is hope. Jesus said that he came that we may have life, not death and destruction, and that we may have it more abundantly. When he said this he was not just referring to having eternal life in heaven as great as that will be. He was also referring to have an abundant life here on this earth.

Paul stated in Romans 7:14-25 that we war against our flesh and our sin has brought us into captivity. 14 For we know that the law in spiritual: but I am carnal, sold under sin.

15 For that which I do I allow not: for what I would, that do I not; but what I hate, that do I.
16 If then I do that which I would not, I consent unto the law that is good.
17 Now then it is no more I that do it, but sin that dwelleth in me.
18 For I know that in me (that is, in my flesh) dwelleth no good thing: for to will is present with me; but how to perform that which is good I find not.
19 *For the good that I would I do not: but the evil which I would not, that I do.*
20 Now if I do that I would not, it is no more I that do it, but sin that dwelleth in me.
21 I find then a law, that, when I would do good, evil is present with me.
22 For I delight in the law of God after the inward man:
23 But I see another law in my members, warring against the law of my mind, and bringing me into captivity to the law of sin which is in my members.
24 O wretched man that I am! Who shall deliver me from the body of this death?
25 I thank God through Jesus Christ our Lord. So then with the **mind I myself serve the law of God**; but **with the flesh the law of sin**.
KJV

Then Paul goes on to tell us the answer to the captivity of our sin in Romans 8:1-6.

1 There is therefore now no condemnation to them which are in Christ Jesus, who walk not after the flesh, but after the Spirit.
2 **For the law of the Spirit of life in Christ Jesus hath made me free from the law of sin and death.**
3 For what the law could not do, in that it was weak through the flesh, **God sending His own Son in the likeness of sinful flesh, and for sin, condemned sin in the flesh:**
4 That the righteousness of the law might be fulfilled in us, who walk not after the flesh, but after the Spirit.
5 For they that are after the flesh do mind the things of the Spirit.
6 For to be **carnally minded** is **death**; but to be **spiritually minded** is **life** and **peace**.
KJV

I hope that by now you get and understanding that Satan and his demonic angels and the sin that they try to trap people into is the source of the problems when it comes to death, destruction and despair. And *that* is what drug addictions are; *death, destruction and despair.* As we go through the remainder of this book, we will look at how the Bible says to deal with these powers, how to combat them and how to defeat them. First, I want to take another look at addictions for a minute. I want to make sure that we have a total understanding about addictions. **According to the Bible** they are not a genetic disorder, disease or anything else except what the Bible says they are.

Do you ever wonder why a person that has a bad habit they cannot overcome? Why a smoker says, "Quitting is easy, I've done it several times," only to continue smoking. Why overweight people have a hard time losing and keeping off the weight. Why an alcoholic can not quit. Why a drug addict can not wait to find their next "fix". People in the world today are being overcome with this spirit of Addiction. Just refer back to Romans 7:19 where Paul talks about not doing the things that he knows he should and doing the things he knows he shouldn't. But there is hope, refer back to Romans 8:2-6. Again, addiction is a force that transforms the spirit and then overcomes a person in the flesh and spirit and can not be over come in the flesh alone.

All addictions are based on the same thing whether they are addictions to food, alcohol, drugs, sex and pornography, money, power, or anything that keeps a complete rule over you in order to destroy your life. The addiction to alcohol, drugs or pornography is just as strong as the lack of will power to stay away from fatty food, junk food or a soda. Many people do not identify with the thoughts of an addict because they do not categorize themselves as addicted to anything. If people would think about the one thing that gives them comfort, whether it be a favorite food, music, television show, or whatever thing that they can not live without. It is the same spirit that affects the drug or alcohol addict because that is where they get their temporary comfort. Think about the last time you went on a diet and the battle that you fought within yourself. This is the same kind of battle that a person with an alcohol, drug or pornography addiction fights every second of every hour of every day of their life.

People become addicted to food and cannot overcome the addiction. What about the lack of willpower in this country alone. The diet industry is a multibillion dollar industry because of this.

Look at what the Bible says about fear and then we will look at how it relates to addictions.

1 John 4:18 states this;

18   There is no fear in love; but perfect love casteth out fear: because fear hath torment. He that feareth is not made perfect in love.
KJV

The spirit of addiction feeds from fear and the torment associated. Addictions are fear dependant because where there is **torment** there is *fear* and vice versa. People with addictions become fearful that they will remain in torment without any relief or comfort. Remember when you went off of that diet and said, "I'll just be fat and happy!" It is the same spirit of fear, just mix this fear with the chemicals of drug or alcohol addiction and when they get their "fix", they get temporary relief. This relief is only temporary, so soon after they are looking for their next "fix". Then when they run out of money, they begin to slide even further into this trap by stealing or doing anything they can to get their next fix.

The relief or comfort that they are trying to find is two tiered. The first is an escape from the realities of this world. The second and most important is the void in their life that only God can fill. But by accepting Jesus as their savior they can fill this void and find refuge in him

Have you ever seen a water whirlpool? White water rapid riders know to stay away from the spiraling water of a whirlpool, because if they get sucked in, there is very little chance they can get out alive. It is the same thing with these powerful addictions. We have to remember that each one of these people involved in this mess, the user, the dealer and the maker has a soul. And once they get trapped in the addiction whirlpool there is a soul that can either be saved or lost. But, praise be to God almighty that through His Son, Jesus we have power to break this stronghold.

Please do not misunderstand me when we talk about the spirit of addiction. I am not speaking of a certain demon or necessarily saying that all persons afflicted with addictions are possessed by demons at all. What I am trying to convey is that there *are* spiritual demonic influences that assist Satan to help him gain control of a person and one of the ways he does this is through drug addiction. These forces may seem ever so subtle at first by telling them that it is okay to try this, you will not get hooked. These forces say, it is okay to sell a little bit just to make some extra money, every body else is doing the same thing. These are the lies that we have spoken about. It starts small then builds a little at a time. Then finally Satan gets *total control* over their lives *and spirit*. Their spirit then becomes polluted with the sins that accompany drug addiction, in turn giving them a "spirit of addiction", that separates them from their friends, family and God.

2

Basis—The Will of God.

Before we get into this subject, I want to interject that I totally believe in the sovereignty and providence of God. God, our Heavenly Father has the power and the right to do anything he wants in the universe or elsewhere. However, when God created this world, he set things in a certain order and he does not and has not deviated from them. In the book if Genesis, God gave to man, his creation, dominion over the earth. To have dominion, means to dominate over it or control everything in it. God set in order seed time and harvest time, where there is a certain time to plant seeds and to reap harvests. There are many other things that have been set in order by the sovereignty of God as well. Further, I believe that God has a master plan for this world and each of us. But we must allow him to work in us and I will elaborate on this momentarily. With that being said we can continue.

Through many years of wrong religious teaching, we have somehow came to a conclusion that God created mankind to be some type of puppet that he plays with on a string. Wrong religious teaching tells us that God is in complete control of all of us, causing us to have adversity hit us directly in the face, and that we are powerless to do anything about it. Sayings such as "you never know what God is going to do", or "when it is your time to go, there is nothing we can do about it", cause us to concede that we are helpless in this earth to change things. The *true* Word of God tells us that God created man in His own (God's) image. The *true* Word of God tells us that God has given us a choice in this life to make our own decisions and affect our own destiny in this life. Let us look at what Deuteronomy 30 has to say about choosing the right pathways in life.

Deut 30:15-31:1

15 See, I have set before thee this day *life* and *good*, and *death* and *evil*;
16 In that I command thee this day to love the LORD thy God, to walk in his ways, and to keep his commandments and his statutes and his judgments, that thou mayest live and multiply: and the LORD thy God shall bless thee in the land whither thou goest to possess it.
17 But if thine heart turn away, so that thou wilt not hear, but shalt be drawn away, and worship other gods, and serve them;
18 I denounce unto you this day, that ye shall surely perish, and that ye shall not prolong your days upon the land, whither thou passest over Jordan to go to possess it.
19 I call heaven and earth to record this day against you, that I have set before you life and death, blessing and cursing: ***therefore choose life, that both thou and thy seed may live:***
20 That thou mayest love the LORD thy God, and that thou mayest obey his voice, and that thou mayest cleave unto him: for he is thy life, and the length of thy days: that thou mayest dwell in the land which the LORD sware unto thy fathers, to Abraham, to Isaac, and to Jacob, to give them.
KJV

Now, having read that passage of scripture straight from the Bible, it sounds to me that God wants and allows us, through his sovereignty, to make the right or wrong decisions in life, and that by choosing and making the *right decisions*, we can have a good life on this earth.

There are Christian teachings that will argue that "the Old Testament is not for us so we do not go by anything that it says". That religious philosophy discussion will not be argued in this book. The point that I want to make here is that the Old Testament is relevant for our understanding of God's nature and his intentions for us as mankind.

Look at this; if God was in complete control of our lives, no one would perish because that is not what God would have for us. But the Bible does not say that, it says for each of us to *choose*. Let me ask you a serious question on this; If God is in control of everything, where do we get the right to punish crime or wickedness in the world. Scripturally, there could be no reward deserved for obedience to God. Neither could there be any penalty for rebellion or disobedience. Do not misunderstand my point here, we definitely want to let God have control of our lives, but my point is that by turning our lives over to Jesus, then consulting God in prayer and studying His Word, we choose to allow Him to influence the choices we make everyday. This is how we let God have control of our lives.

With that said, we can now discuss the notion that sometimes we get caught up in what is "the will of God". If we would open our hearts, eyes and our Bibles, we can find the will of God concerning the futures of every man, woman and child are found right there in plain print. In this situation along with others, the will of God concerning this is found in II Peter 3:9.

9   The Lord is not slack concerning his promise, as some men count slackness; but is longsuffering to us-ward, *not willing that any should perish, but that all should come to repentance.*
KJV

The key here is willing. By reading this passage, we can take from it that it is **not God's Will** that anyone should perish, but that all should come to repentance. People that are in these bondages of addiction can not come to repentance until the bonds of addiction are broken. It is this passage in which God has enlightened me on that says if we will put this "Word of God" as our number one weapon in the fight of breaking the spirit of addiction, pray about it, focus on it, stand on it, believe on it, it WILL help us move the mountain of addiction.

Let us review this a little further. If this passage of scripture is correct, then it would be safe to say that it is God's will for all to repent so none would perish. And if it is God's will that none perish, then when we pray for and agree with God's Word, we are truly in the Will of God. And when we truly get in the Will of God, there is no devil anywhere that can stop the Will of God from coming to fruition. But the key is in our hands.

3

Intercessory Prayer

James 5:16

Confess your faults one to another, and pray one for another, that ye may be healed. **The effectual fervent prayer of a righteous man availeth much.** KJV

There is a tool which we have that is often way underestimated, prayer. It is usually an afterthought for events. Have you ever heard the term, "all we can do is pray", it is usually met with and said with an exasperating type of despair. What we need to focus on is something called Intercessory Prayer. Through Intercessory Prayer we are standing in the gap for the person that may not have anyone to pray for them or are unwilling or unknowing enough to pray for themselves. We are utilizing ***our faith*** in the Blood of Jesus that was shed for all of us, to fight a spiritual warfare on their behalf. In my experience with Intercessory Prayer, I have had have family members tell me, "Please do not quit praying for me". Even though they were not yet able to come to grips with their problem yet, they knew what the true solution was.

Where do we get the right to intercede on the behalf of other people, you may ask? Let us look at I Timothy 2:1-6.

1   I exhort therefore, that first of all, supplications, prayers, ***intercessions***, and giving of thanks, ***be made for all men;***

2   For kings, and for all that are in authority; that we may lead a quiet and peaceable life in all godliness and honesty.

3   for this is good and acceptable in the sight of God our Saviour;

4   Who will have all men to be saved, and to come unto the knowledge of the truth.

5   For there is one God, and one mediator between God and men, the man Christ Jesus;

6   Who gave himself a ransom for all, to be testified in due time.
KJV

Verse one will leave little doubt about whether we have a right or maybe even an obligation to intercede in prayer for others. Actually, if we go back a little further in the Bible, we do have a duty to pray for others. Let us take a look at 1 Samuel 12:20-25.

20   And Samuel said unto the people, Fear not: ye have done all this wickedness: yet turn not aside from following the LORD, but serve the LORD with all your heart;

21   And turn ye not aside: for then should ye go after vain things, which cannot profit nor deliver; for they are vain.

22   For the LORD will not forsake his people for his great name's sake: because it hath pleased the LORD to make you his people.

23   Moreover as for me, **God forbid that I should sin against the LORD in ceasing to pray for you**: but I will teach you the good and the right way:

24   Only fear the LORD, and serve him in truth with all your heart: for consider how great things he hath done for you.

25   But if ye shall still do wickedly, ye shall be consumed, both ye and your king.
KJV

Samuel called failing to pray for others a sin against God. Jesus led by example going out and praying for people. He even said in Matthew 5:44

44   But I say unto you, Love your enemies, bless them that curse you, do good to them that hate you, and **pray** for them which **despitefully use you, and persecute you;**
KJV

There are many examples of people in the Bible who prayed for others, let us look at Daniel 9:20,

20   And whiles I was speaking, and praying, and confessing my sin **and the sin of my people Israel**, and presenting my supplication before the LORD my God for the holy mountain of my God;
KJV

1 Sam 1:22-2:1

22 But Hannah went not up; for she said unto her husband, I will not go up until the child be weaned, and then I will bring him, that he may appear before the LORD, and there abide for ever

23 And Elkanah her husband said unto her, Do what seemeth thee good; tarry until thou have weaned him; only the LORD establish his word. So the woman abode, and gave her son suck until she weaned him.

24 And when she had weaned him, she took him up with her, with three bullocks, and one ephah of flour, and a bottle of wine, and brought him unto the house of the LORD in Shiloh: and the child was young.

25 And they slew a bullock, and brought the child to Eli.

26 And she said, Oh my lord, as thy soul liveth, my lord, I am the woman that stood by thee here, praying unto the LORD.

27 *For this child I prayed; and the LORD hath given me my petition which I asked of him:*

28 Therefore also I have lent him to the LORD; as long as he liveth he shall be lent to the LORD. And he worshipped the LORD there.

KJV

Before we leave this thought, let us look at what intercessions Jesus made and still makes for us today.

Isaiah 53:12 states;

12 Therefore will I divide him a portion with the great, and he shall divide the spoil with the strong; because he hath poured out his soul unto death: and he was numbered with the transgressors; and he bare the sin of many, and *made intercession* for the transgressors.

KJV

Hebrews 4:14-16 states;

14 Seeing then that we have *a great high priest*, that is passed into the heavens, Jesus the Son of God, let us hold fast our profession.

15 For we have not an high priest which cannot be touched with the feeling of our infirmities; but was in all points tempted like as we are, yet without sin.

16 Let us therefore come boldly unto the throne of grace, that we may obtain mercy, *and find grace to help in time of need.*

KJV

God *wants* to help us in our time of need and will if we will trust and believe in him.

Hebrews 7:23-25 states;

23 And they truly were many priests, because they were not suffered to continue by reason of death:
24 But this man, because he continueth ever, hath an unchangeable priesthood.
25 Wherefore he is able also to save them to the uttermost that come unto God by him, seeing he ever liveth to **_make intercession for them_**.
KJV

1 John 2:1

2:1 My little children, these things write I unto you, that ye sin not. And if any man sin, we have an **_advocate_** with the Father, Jesus Christ the righteous:
KJV

Now when we put all that together and get the proper perspective on those scriptures, we can see that Jesus is our advocate and our high priest who made and still continuously makes intercession for us. With that being said, we now know that Jesus intercedes for us and we should intercede for others. This is a vital key in breaking the spirit of addiction.

4

Uniting in Prayer

Unity is a powerful thing, it does not matter whether it is on a football team, a job or dealing with spiritual matter, again, unity is a powerful thing. The Bible gives examples and is clear on this. Do you remember the "Tower of Babel" and how they were so determined to work together to build a building that reached into the heavens? They were on their way, but what they did not know was that they were way ahead of their time. For their own safety, God had to put an end to their construction plans. Let us take a look at Genesis 11;

Genesis 11:5-6

5   And the LORD came down to see the city and the tower, which the children of men builded.
6   And the LORD said, Behold, **the people is one**, and they have all one language; and this they begin to do: *and now nothing will be restrained from them, which they have imagined to do.*
KJV

Let us look at verse 6 in the NIV translation;

Gen 11:6

6   The LORD said, "If as one people speaking the same language they have begun to do this, then ***nothing they plan to do will be impossible for them.***
NIV

Wow! When these people were in agreement together, working as one unit, uniting their faith and vision, ***nothing*** was going to be impossible for them. Now that is power!

The Bible tells us in several places that we as Christians should unite together. Jesus Himself tells us in Matthew 18 that we are very strong when we are united together. The term "United We Stand, Divided We Fall" really comes into play here. Let us look at what Matthew 18:19-20 states;

19   Again I say unto you, that if ***two of you shall agree*** on earth as touching any thing that ***they shall ask, it shall be done*** for them of my Father which is in heaven.
20   For where two or three are gathered together in my name, there am I in the midst of them.
KJV

We need to understand that there is power and strength in numbers.

The Bible is also very clear about when we as Christians begin to get in the Will of God, unite and believe on His word, the prayers that we ask of Him ***will*** be answered. Let us look at what the gospel of Johns says;

John 14:11-14

11   Believe me that I am in the Father, and the Father in me: or else believe me for the very works' sake.
12   Verily, verily, I say unto you, ***He that believeth on me,*** the works that I do shall he do also; and greater works than these shall he do; because I go unto my Father.
13   And ***whatsoever ye shall ask in my name, that will I do,*** that the Father may be glorified in the Son.
14   If ye shall ask any thing in my name, I will do it.
KJV

John 15:7

7   If ye abide in me, and my words abide in you, ye **shall ask** what ye will, and **it shall be done** unto you.
KJV

John 15:16

16 Ye have not chosen me, but I have chosen you, and ordained you, that ye should go and bring forth fruit, and that your fruit should remain: that **whatsoever ye shall ask of the Father in my name**, he may give it you.
KJV

John 16:22-24

22 And ye now therefore have sorrow: but I will see you again, and your heart shall rejoice, and your joy no man taketh from you.
23 And in that day ye shall ask me nothing. Verily, verily, I say unto you, Whatsoever ye shall ask the Father in my name, he will give it you.
24 Hitherto have ye asked nothing in my name: **ask, and ye shall receive,** that your joy may be full.
KJV

The power or authority given in these scriptures is not to be mistreated or abused. It is given to Christians so that they can help usher in God's Will on this earth. Let us look at what the book of James has to say;

James 4:3

3   Ye ask, and receive not, because ye ask amiss, that ye may consume it upon your lusts.
KJV

We should not be self centered individuals that are only concerned about how things are going to affect us. In order for us to receive the petitions that we ask for, we must focus the upon God's kingdom in order for our prayers to be answered. Matthew 6:33 has it this way;

Matt 6:33

But seek ye first the kingdom of God, and his righteousness; and all these things shall be added unto you.
KJV

By first arranging our priorities in line with the Kingdom of God and his right standing, then we can get the results that we desire for or family and friends.

5

Faith in the Word of God

Faith is something that has been confused distorted and completely misunderstood by many Christians. Faith in my opinion is simple. Believe entirely in God's Word. If God's Word says it, as a Christian, we ***must*** believe it. Unfortunately many Christians do not know what the Word says about a certain situation. Most Christians attend church, give to the offering and are good people. This is the way I was until; I started opening my Bible, reading and praying for wisdom. But unfortunately a lot of Christians do not open their Bible to find out what God's word truly says instead they just get enough Word on Sunday to get them through the week. We as Christians must get into an intense study and find out what is being said in this great book.

When we then find out what is being said, we must believe it. Let us look at what Mark 11 says;

Mark 11:22-26

22 And Jesus answering saith unto them, ***Have faith in God.***
23 For verily I say unto you, That whosoever shall say unto this mountain, Be thou removed, and be thou cast into the sea; ***and shall not doubt in his heart,*** but shall believe that those things which he saith shall come to pass; he shall have whatsoever he saith.
24 Therefore I say unto you, What things soever ye desire, when ye pray, believe that ye receive them, and ye shall have them.

25 And when ye stand praying, forgive, if ye have ought against any: that your Father also which is in heaven may forgive you your trespasses.

26 But if ye do not forgive, neither will your Father which is in heaven forgive your trespasses.

KJV

Having faith in God has been the common theme in the entire Bible. If we do not believe God's Word about being able to break the spirit of addiction, how can we believe it for our salvation? There are instances in the Bible that demonstrate that Jesus power on this earth was limited because the people he was dealing with did not believe in him or his healing power. Matthew 13:54-58 shows us this;

54 And when he was come into his own country, he taught them in their synagogue, insomuch that they were astonished, and said, Whence hath this man this wisdom, and these mighty works?

55 Is not this the carpenter's son? is not his mother called Mary? and his brethren, James, and Joses, and Simon, and Judas?

56 And his sisters, are they not all with us? Whence then hath this man all these things?

57 And they were *offended* in him. But Jesus said unto them, A prophet is not without honour, save in his own country, and in his own house.

58 *And he did not many mighty works there because of their **unbelief**.*

KJV

These people were at first astonished by what Jesus was teaching them, and then they became offended. I would be safe to point out at this point that if you begin to do what is outlined in God's Word, through this book, and start believing and expecting for people to be delivered, then you will eventually offend someone by doing this. This does not mean you are doing anything wrong, many people in the world will just not understand, until they are enlightened. But do not get discouraged just believe in God's plan.

Faith in God's word is not anymore plain than in the book of Hebrews. Hebrews 11 is "the Faith Hall of Fame Chapter" in the Bible. Let us take a look.

Heb 11:1-12:1

11:1 Now *faith* is the substance of things hoped for, the evidence of things not seen.

2 For by it the elders obtained a good report.

3 Through *faith* we understand that the worlds were framed by the word of God, so that things which are seen were not made of things which do appear.

4   By *faith* Abel offered unto God a more excellent sacrifice than Cain, by which he obtained witness that he was righteous, God testifying of his gifts: and by it he being dead yet speaketh.

5   By *faith* Enoch was translated that he should not see death; and was not found, because God had translated him: for before his translation he had this testimony, that he pleased God.

6   ***But without faith it is impossible to please him: for he that cometh to God must believe that he is, and that he is a rewarder of them that diligently seek him.***

7   By *faith* Noah, being warned of God of things not seen as yet, moved with fear, prepared an ark to the saving of his house; by the which he condemned the world, and became heir of the righteousness which is by *faith*.

8   By *faith* Abraham, when he was called to go out into a place which he should after receive for an inheritance, obeyed; and he went out, not knowing whither he went.

9   By *faith* he sojourned in the land of promise, as in a strange country, dwelling in tabernacles with Isaac and Jacob, the heirs with him of the same promise:

10   For he looked for a city which hath foundations, whose builder and maker is God.

11   Through *faith* also Sara herself received strength to conceive seed, and was delivered of a child when she was past age, because she judged him faithful who had promised.

12   Therefore sprang there even of one, and him as good as dead, so many as the stars of the sky in multitude, and as the sand which is by the sea shore innumerable.

13   These all died in *faith*, not having received the promises, but having seen them afar off, and were persuaded of them, and embraced them, and confessed that they were strangers and pilgrims on the earth.

14   For they that say such things declare plainly that they seek a country.

15   And truly, if they had been mindful of that country from whence they came out, they might have had opportunity to have returned.

16   But now they desire a better country, that is, an heavenly: wherefore God is not ashamed to be called their God: for he hath prepared for them a city.

17   By *faith* Abraham, when he was tried, offered up Isaac: and he that had received the promises offered up his only begotten son,

18   Of whom it was said, That in Isaac shall thy seed be called:

19   Accounting that God was able to raise him up, even from the dead; from whence also he received him in a figure.

20   By *faith* Isaac blessed Jacob and Esau concerning things to come.

21   By *faith* Jacob, when he was a dying, blessed both the sons of Joseph; and worshipped, leaning upon the top of his staff.

22 By *faith* Joseph, when he died, made mention of the departing of the children of Israel; and gave commandment concerning his bones.

23 By *faith* Moses, when he was born, was hid three months of his parents, because they saw he was a proper child; and they were not afraid of the king's commandment.

24 By *faith* Moses, when he was come to years, refused to be called the son of Pharaoh's daughter;

25 Choosing rather to suffer affliction with the people of God, than to enjoy the pleasures of sin for a season;

26 Esteeming the reproach of Christ greater riches than the treasures in Egypt: for he had respect unto the recompence of the reward.

27 By *faith* he forsook Egypt, not fearing the wrath of the king: for he endured, as seeing him who is invisible.

28 Through *faith* he kept the passover, and the sprinkling of blood, lest he that destroyed the firstborn should touch them.

29 By *faith* they passed through the Red sea as by dry land: which the Egyptians assaying to do were drowned.

30 By *faith* the walls of Jericho fell down, after they were compassed about seven days.

31 By *faith* the harlot Rahab perished not with them that believed not, when she had received the spies with peace.

32 And what shall I more say? for the time would fail me to tell of Gedeon, and of Barak, and of Samson, and of Jephthae; of David also, and Samuel, and of the prophets:

33 Who through *faith* subdued kingdoms, wrought righteousness, obtained promises, stopped the mouths of lions,

34 Quenched the violence of fire, escaped the edge of the sword, out of weakness were made strong, waxed valiant in fight, turned to flight the armies of the aliens.

35 Women received their dead raised to life again: and others were tortured, not accepting deliverance; that they might obtain a better resurrection:

36 And others had trial of cruel mockings and scourgings, yea, moreover of bonds and imprisonment:

37 They were stoned, they were sawn asunder, were tempted, were slain with the sword: they wandered about in sheepskins and goatskins; being destitute, afflicted, tormented;

38 (Of whom the world was not worthy:) they wandered in deserts, and in mountains, and in dens and caves of the earth.

39 And these all, having obtained a good report through *faith*, received not the promise:

40 God having provided some better thing for us, that they without us should not be made perfect.

KJV

Now I know that was a lot of scripture to digest, but it is important for you to understand, ***do not just take someone else's word or opinion for granted***. You need to ***know what faith*** in God ***has done*** and ***can do*** in your situation.

Before we move on, let us take a quick look at what the Word of God says about . . . . The Word of God.

2 Tim 3:14-4:1

14   But continue thou in the things which thou hast learned and hast been assured of, knowing of whom thou hast learned them;
15   And that from a child thou hast known the ***holy scriptures, which are able to make thee wise unto salvation through faith which is in Christ Jesus.***
16   ***All scripture is given by inspiration of God***, and is ***profitable for doctrine***, for ***reproof***, for ***correction***, for ***instruction in righteousness***:
17   That the man of God may be perfect, ***throughly furnished unto all good works.***
KJV

First, let us look a verse 15; it refers to the Bible as Holy Scriptures which can give us wisdom (knowledge) for salvation through faith in Jesus. Then we find out that **ALL** scripture is inspired by God and that this inspired word is useful for teaching, rebuking, correcting and training. And finally we see that if we continue in what we have learned (reference verse 14) and will learn, we can be equipped for every good work. Now link that with what we discussed in learning the will of God and we ***will*** be able to move those mountains or addictions.

6

Job's lack of faith in God.

After speaking about having faith in God, let us look at what can happen when good, Godly people do not put complete faith in God. The book of Job is a very interesting book, which allows us a good look at a man of God that the Bible calls perfect and upright.

Job 1:1-5

1:1 There was a man in the land of Uz, whose name was Job; and that man was perfect and upright, and one that feared God, and eschewed evil.
2 And there were born unto him seven sons and three daughters.
3 His substance also was seven thousand sheep, and three thousand camels, and five hundred yoke of oxen, and five hundred she asses, and a very great household; so that this man was the greatest of all the men of the east.
4 And his sons went and feasted in their houses, every one his day; and sent and called for their three sisters to eat and to drink with them.
5 And it was so, when the days of their feasting were gone about, that Job sent and sanctified them, and rose up early in the morning, and offered burnt offerings according to the number of them all: for ***Job said, It may be that my sons have sinned, and cursed God in their hearts. Thus did Job continually.*** KJV

It is in verse 5 that we find that Job was concerned about his children. So concerned that he continually gave offerings for them. That sounds okay, but after

Job prayed for them and gave an offering for them, all that was needed for them to be protected was for Job to believe in God's Word. The problem came when Job did not believe God had the situation under control.

Paul gave us an example of what to do in this situation in Ephesians 6

Eph 6:13

13 Wherefore take unto you the whole armour of God, that ye may be able to withstand in the evil day, and having done all, *to stand*.
KJV

What are we to stand on, the promises that God made to us in this Word of his. You see here, I am not accusing Job of not doing anything, he did all that he knew how to do, but he allowed *fear* to creep in and disrupt his faith in God. Let us look further at Job.

Job 1:7-12

7   And the LORD said unto Satan, Whence comest thou? Then Satan answered the LORD, and said, From going to and fro in the earth, and from walking up and down in it.
8   And the LORD said unto Satan, Hast thou considered my servant Job, that there is none like him in the earth, a perfect and an upright man, one that feareth God, and escheweth evil?
9   Then Satan answered the LORD, and said, Doth Job fear God for nought?
10 Hast not thou made an hedge about him, and about his house, and about all that he hath on every side? thou hast blessed the work of his hands, and his substance is increased in the land.
11 But put forth thine hand now, and touch all that he hath, and he will curse thee to thy face.
12 And the LORD said unto Satan, Behold, all that he hath is in thy power; only upon himself put not forth thine hand. So Satan went forth from the presence of the LORD.
KJV

Here, God and Satan have conversation about Job. Satan is roaming around on the earth as he is still to this day, looking for someone to attack. God knows what Satan is up to and confronts him about it. To Satan, Job appears completely protected, but Satan does not know about Job's fear regarding his children. Then here is the debatable part of the book of Job. It has been taught that God allowed Satan to destroy Job. Does that truly sound like a God of love that gave his own Son for us, that does not want any of us to perish? It does not, does it? But by understanding what we allow fear to mix in with, **God has to allow things to happen,** because we unknowingly choose to allow fear in the picture. Let us look further at this. In verse 12 God says to Satan, "Behold, all that he hath is in thy power", or look, all that he has is in reach of you. How and why did God say that to Satan? God never lies, not to you, me or even Satan. God knew that there was a crack in Job's "hedge", but he could not lie about it, so he told Satan the truth. But God also told Satan not to kill Job. So, we then know that Satan afflicted Job with many things. Here is the next relevant scripture that we want to reference to in Job, and that is in the third chapter.

Job 3:23-26

23 Why is light given to a man whose way is hid, and whom God hath hedged in?
24 For my sighing cometh before I eat, and my roarings are poured out like the waters.
25 For the thing which I greatly **feared** is come upon me, and that which **I was afraid** of is come unto me.
26 **I was not in safety, neither had I rest, neither was I quiet**; yet trouble came.
KJV

It is by Job's own admission that he was afraid and allowed fear into the situation. In Job's defense, he knew God's love, blessings and protection, but he let his eyes get off of God's promises and get on his children's situation. As we continue learning how to break the spirit of addiction, we **must** focus on God's word and Jesus' sacrifice on the cross, not on the situation that we are standing in prayer for.

As for this interpretation of Job's plight, do not take my word for it; do not take anyone else's word for it. Read the book of Job slowly and then pray about it and let God speak to you about it, He will give wisdom to those who ask for it.

One can understand what Job was going through. But, when he began to worry about his children, fear crept in and opened the door. What does the Bible say about worry, let's look;

Phil 4:6-7

6 **Be careful for nothing**, but in every thing by prayer and supplication with thanksgiving let your requests be made known unto God.
7 And the **peace of God**, which passeth all understanding, **shall keep your hearts and minds through Christ Jesus.**
KJV

1 Peter 5:6-7

6   Humble yourselves therefore under the mighty hand of God, that he may exalt
     you in due time:
7   ***Casting all your care upon him***; for he careth for you.
KJV

This is something that is so hard for us to do in this day and time, but we must
trust in God's promises and instructions in His Word. Especially as our children grow
older in time, Satan attempts to do the same thing with us as he did with Job. He
wants to take our faith away and get us into a position of worry or "being anxious"
as other translations of the Bible have it. But, God's Word instructs us to cast our
cares (concerns, worries) upon Him.

7

Understanding God's love for us.

1 John 4:4-12

4 Ye are of God, little children, and have overcome them: because **greater is he that is in you, than he that is in the world**.
5 They are of the world: therefore speak they of the world, and the world heareth them.
6 We are of God: he that knoweth God heareth us; he that is not of God heareth not us. Hereby know we the spirit of truth, and the spirit of error.
7 Beloved, let us love one another: for **love is of God**; and every one that loveth is born of God, and knoweth God.
8 He that loveth not knoweth not God; for **God is love.**
9 In this was manifested the love of God toward us, because that God sent his only begotten Son into the world, that we might live through him.
10 Herein is love, not that we loved God, but that he loved us, and sent his Son to be the propitiation for our sins.
11 Beloved, **if God so loved us, we ought also to love one another**.
12 No man hath seen God at any time. If we love one another, God dwelleth in us, and his love is perfected in us.
KJV

I would like to start this chapter by saying that I hope you are beginning to get stirred up within yourself and the light in your spirit is beginning to come on. Verse 4 says that greater is he that is in us than he that is in the world. Who is the one in the world, the devil, Satan, or whatever it is you refer to him by, is the one referred to here. There are so many promises of reassurance, uplifting and pictures of triumph of the Power of God overcoming evil in God's Word that if you will refocus your thinking and reprogram your mind the Word will revolutionize your life. Unfortunately we are surrounded by doom and gloom so much that it affects our thinking. Have you ever heard the expression, "that's just my luck", it is usually followed by some sort of negativity that associated every thing we do with expecting something bad. Well, let me tell you that the Word of God associates believing on God's Word with positive things and blessings. Christians that associate themselves with some type of force called "luck" are not speaking the Word of God. In fact the word or reference to the word "luck" or a derivative of this word is **NOT** in the Bible. The Bible speaks of choosing blessings or curses, based entirely upon walking with or without God. (For clarity refer back to chapter 1 were we discussed Deuteronomy 30).

Please do not take my word for it, go and look in any Bible concordance to see for yourself.

Let us get back to the Love of God. Verse 7 says that Love is of God and verse 8 says that God is Love. It is clear that if we are going to stand in intercession for people, we are going to have to settle some things first. I hear people talk about giving up on their friends and loved ones because these friends and loved ones have put them through so much. The word says to forgive and to love. We must remember that the person we are standing in for *is not the problem*. The problem is the spirit of addiction that has them captive. I hope you are starting to see this by now. We must love these people unconditionally, period! Not looking at the outside of them, but looking at them on the inside, like God did for us when He sent His own Son, Jesus to be a sacrifice for *us*. Let us take a look at John 3.

John 3:16-17

16 For God so loved the world, that he gave his only begotten Son, that *whosoever* believeth in him should not perish, but have everlasting life.
17 For God sent not his Son into the world to condemn the world; but *that the world through him might be saved.*
KJV

These are some of the most remembered and quoted word of the Bible. But what we need to keep in mind is that Jesus came for the world and the "who-so-evers". The condition of the world was and is sin, but God, the Heavenly Father sent Jesus, His only Son, to save a world that was in a sin stricken atmosphere and transform the world, regardless of the world's present condition. This image should be how we look at those people we are standing for. There is a great example of this type of love in the Bible; in the next chapter we will take a good look at it.

8

The "Prodigal Son"

Luke 15:11-24

11 And he said, a certain man had two sons:

12 And the younger of them said to his father, Father, give me the portion of goods that falleth to me. And he divided unto them his living.

13 And not many days after the younger son gathered all together, and took his journey into a far country, and there wasted his substance *with riotous living.*

14 And when he had spent all, there arose a mighty famine in that land; and he began to be *in want.*

15 And he went and joined himself to a citizen of that country; and he sent him into his fields to feed swine.

16 And he would fain have filled his belly *with the husks that the swine did eat*: and no man gave unto him.

17 *And when he came to himself,* he said, How many hired servants of my father's have bread enough and to spare, and I perish with hunger!

18 I will arise and go to my father, and will say unto him, *Father, I have sinned against heaven, and before thee,*

19 And am no more worthy to be called thy son: make me as one of thy hired servants.

20 And he arose, and came to his father. But when he was yet a great way off, his father saw him, and had compassion, and ran, and fell on his neck, and kissed him.

21 And the son said unto him, Father, I have sinned against heaven, and in thy sight, and am no more worthy to be called thy son.

22 But the father said to his servants, Bring forth the best robe, and put it on him; and put a ring on his hand, and shoes on his feet:

23 And bring hither the fatted calf, and kill it; and let us eat, and be merry:

24 *For this my son was dead, and is alive again; he was lost, and is found*. And they began to be merry.
KJV

Here is a person that wanted to go out on his own to seek his own way in life. He could have been lead by God and been prosperous as his father was if only he had chosen the right path, but the word says that he "wasted his substance with riotous living". Then he began to be in need, so eventually he found himself eating husks with the hogs. His life took such an enormous decline that he was not even existing like a person should. Capture that image in your mind, then take that same image and compare it with that of the drug dependant person that you have in mind. Striking similarities aren't they. That person also has hit rock bottom and is not even living as most animals do in our society. But there is hope, let us continue.

Verse 17 states that this person "came to himself". When a person does not want help, they *will not* come to the realization of the dire situation they are in. But when they get to a point that their attention can be had, they can realize that there is food in their Father's house. Pay attention here because this is an important part in breaking the spirit of addiction. This person "came to himself" and returned to his father's residence and repented of his mistakes. Look at the love that his father had for the son that had once been lost;

Luke 15:20

But when he was yet a great way off, his father saw him, and had *compassion*, and ran, and fell on his neck, and kissed him.
KJV

Luke 15:22-24

But the father said to his servants, Bring forth the best robe, and put it on him; and put a ring on his hand, and shoes on his feet:

23 And bring hither the fatted calf, and kill it; and let us eat, and be merry:
24 *For this my son was dead, and is alive again; he was lost, and is found*.
KJV

That is the love that we need to have in order for our prayers to be heard and answered. Anything less will not qualify for success assured. Start imagining the day, capturing the vision of the first Thanksgiving or Christmas you have where all is finally well in your household, according to God's Word it can and will happen if we will believe. We will talk more about capturing the vision later.

9

Pray for wisdom

We need to understand that knowledge of the truth in any situation we deal with in this life gives us power. How? You may ask, well if we have knowledge, we will not be deceived by lies or misunderstandings. How can we obtain wisdom? Well first we need to pray and ask God for wisdom in this and/or any endeavor that we are undertaking. If you study the Bible closely concerning wisdom, it will become clear that wisdom is the scriptural answer to any worldly problem. Where we begin to have problems is when we have a lack of knowledge about a situation. Hosea 4 speaks of and gives an account about lack of knowledge; let us take a look;

Hosea 4:6

6   *My people are destroyed for lack of knowledge: because thou hast rejected knowledge*, I will also reject thee, that thou shalt be no priest to me: seeing thou hast forgotten the law of thy God, I will also forget thy children.
KJV

God is telling these people in this account a truth about life. The truth of today is that people are being destroyed by the lies and deception of drug addiction. You see, no one sets out to be an addict. It starts out small and then builds to where these substances take complete control of their lives. If they knew the condition that they would eventually decline to they would not put themselves and their families

44

through "hell on earth". It is the lie they believe that says, "It will not happen to me", but with *true knowledge* they would know that this is a lie from Satan and a snare for them to fall into and bring them into captivity. But unfortunately soon after that first "hit" of whatever it is they get hooked on, it is too late.

The Bible has many scriptures that talk about gaining wisdom; let us look at a few;

Matthew 7:7-11

7   *Ask*, and it shall be *given* you; *seek*, and ye shall *find*; *knock*, and it shall be *opened* unto you:
8   For every one that asketh receiveth; and he that seeketh findeth; and to him that knocketh it shall be opened.
9   Or what man is there of you, whom if his son ask bread, will he give him a stone?
10 Or if he ask a fish, will he give him a serpent?
11 If ye then, being evil, know how to give good gifts unto your children, *how much more shall your Father which is in heaven give good things to them that ask him?*
KJV

Proverbs 1:7

7   The fear of the LORD is the beginning of knowledge: but *fools despise wisdom and instruction*
KJV

Proverbs 2:1-2

2:1 My son, if thou wilt receive my words, and hide my commandments with thee;
2   So that thou *incline thine ear unto wisdom*, and *apply thine heart to understanding*, KJV

Proverbs 2:6-7

6   For *the LORD giveth wisdom*: out of his mouth cometh knowledge and understanding.
7   He *layeth up sound wisdom for the righteous*: he is a buckler to them that walk uprightly.
KJV

Proverbs 2:9-12

9 Then shalt thou understand righteousness, and judgment, and equity; yea, every good path.
10 **When wisdom entereth into thine heart, and knowledge is pleasant unto thy soul;**
11 Discretion shall preserve thee, understanding shall keep thee:
12 To deliver thee from the way of the evil man, from the man that speaketh froward things;
KJV

Proverbs 4:5-7

5 **Get wisdom**, get understanding: **forget it not**; neither decline from the words of my mouth.
6 **Forsake her not, and she shall preserve thee**: love her, and she shall keep thee.
7 Wisdom is the principal thing; therefore **get wisdom**: and with all thy getting get understanding.
KJV

Proverbs 4:10-11

10 Hear, O my son, and receive my sayings; **and the years of thy life shall be many.**
11 I have taught thee in the way of wisdom; I have led thee in right paths.
KJV

Proverbs 9:10-11

10 The fear of the LORD is the **beginning of wisdom**: and the knowledge of the holy is understanding.
11 **For by me thy days shall be multiplied, and the years of thy life shall be increased.**
KJV

James 1:5

5 If any of you lack wisdom, let him **ask** of God, that giveth to all men liberally, and upbraideth not; **and it shall be given him.**
KJV

After reviewing these scriptures, I find it interesting that wisdom is directly related to understanding. I also find it interesting that wisdom and understanding are related to lengthening your days on this earth, did you see that?

There are many scriptures on wisdom and understanding; I suggest that in your studies, you find others that will enhance what we are talking about.

10

Spiritual Combat

By now I hope that you have a good understanding what the basis of this book is about. It is not about my opinion, or interpretation, it is about the Word of God and what it says about breaking through spiritual barriers, in the situation we are dealing with, drug addiction. Once we see what it says and understand it, we can then move on into spiritual battle.

In order for us as Christians to help the captives of our family, friends and the world, we must fight the spiritual battle that Jesus commissioned us to do. This is a battle that can only be attacked and won in the spiritual realm by the proper army of God. Let us look at what Ephesians 6 says;

Ephesians 6:13-17

13 Wherefore take unto you the whole armour of God, that ye may be able to withstand in the evil day, and having done all, to stand.
14 Stand therefore, having your loins girt about with ***truth***, and having on the breastplate of ***righteousness***;
15 And your feet shod with the ***preparation of the gospel of peace;***
16 Above all, taking the shield of ***faith***, wherewith ye shall be able to quench all the fiery darts of the wicked.
17 And take the helmet of ***salvation***, and the ***sword of the Spirit, which is the word of God:***
KJV

Truth, we have talked about the truth, wisdom, understanding and the consequences of not having or knowing them.

Righteousness means to be in right standing with God. Without being in right standing with God our prayers will not be answered, nor can we accomplish anything in the realm of prayer and spiritual battle.

Preparation of the Gospel of Peace, that is what we have been doing, preparing ourselves with the Gospel (good news) that Jesus died for us allowing us to have peace on this earth and that with God all things are possible in our lives.

Faith, we have talked a lot about faith in God's Word and that he will do what he says.

Salvation, We must accept Jesus as our Savior, repenting of our sins and according to your denomination, be baptized in order to receive salvation. The Word says that the effectual prayer of a righteous man availeth much. But, God will not answer the prayers of a sinner; the only prayer that God answers from a sinner is a prayer of repentance. Sin separates us from God and all that he has in store for us. If there is sin in your life, you are separated from God. By being separated from God your prayers just are not going to get results. You must have done the above mentioned in order to be saved, it is only then that your prayers are heard in heaven.

Sword of the Spirit, The sword of the Spirit is the Word of God and we have reviewed several passages of the Word.

Now let us get ready for spiritual combat.

The Training

We need to be in training. Soldiers prepare for combat, for many months and years before entering into the battlefield. We cannot step onto the battlefield without the proper equipment and training and expect to be victorious. We need repetition in our training. We need to be studying the scriptures, confessing the scriptures and believing the scriptures that deal with our situation, just like a weight lifter that gets a little stronger and a little stronger every time he does a repetition. Jesus knew the power of proper preparation and stated this to His disciples in the book of Matthew. Let us take a look;

Matthew 17:14-21

14 And when they were come to the multitude, there came to him a certain man, kneeling down to him, and saying,

15 Lord, have mercy on my son: for he is lunatick, and sore vexed: for ofttimes he falleth into the fire, and oft into the water.

16 And I brought him to thy disciples, and they could not cure him.

17 Then Jesus answered and said, O faithless and perverse generation, how long shall I be with you? how long shall I suffer you? bring him hither to me.

18 And Jesus rebuked the devil; and he departed out of him: and the child was cured from that very hour.

19 Then came the disciples to Jesus apart, and said, Why could not we cast him out?

20 And Jesus said unto them, Because of your unbelief: for verily I say unto you, If ye have faith as a grain of mustard seed, ye shall say unto this mountain, Remove hence to yonder place; and it shall remove; and nothing shall be impossible unto you.

21 *Howbeit this kind goeth not out but by prayer and fasting.*
KJV

In Matthew 17:14-21 a person described as a lunatic was brought to Jesus for help. Some of His disciples had attempted to help Him prior to this, but they were to no avail. Jesus showed them, and us, during this, the importance of preparation. After delivering the subject from a demonic possession, the disciples asked Jesus why they did not have any success. Jesus replies by essentially telling them that they were not prepared enough.

What Jesus was saying was that not only did the disciples need to work on their faith, but they needed "more reps" in their prayer and fasting.

The Uniting

We need to understand that there is power and strength in numbers. If we will catch hold of this and unite together, after our training and equipping, we are a mighty army, ready for spiritual combat.

The Equipping

Again let us look at what Paul writes in the book of Ephesians about the equipment needed.

Ephesians 6:13-18

13 Wherefore take unto you the whole armour of God, that ye may be able to withstand in the evil day, and having done all, to stand.

14 Stand therefore, having your loins girt about with truth, and having on the breastplate of righteousness;

15 And your feet shod with the preparation of the gospel of peace;

16 Above all, taking the shield of faith, wherewith ye shall be able to quench all the fiery darts of the wicked.

17 And take the helmet of salvation, *and the sword of the Spirit, which is the word of God:*

18 Praying always with all prayer and supplication in the Spirit, and watching thereunto with all perseverance and supplication for all saints;

KJV

But, what equipment or weapons are necessary for this battle?

II Corinthians 10:4 states

4 For the weapons of our warfare are not carnal, but *mighty* through God to *the pulling down of strong holds.*

KJV

That is exactly what drug addictions are, strongholds of Satan that he has on people in order to keep them from fulfilling the calling that each person has in their life.

Hebrews 4:12 states

12 For the word of God is quick, and powerful, and sharper that any twoedged sword, piercing even to the dividing asunder of soul and spirit, and of the joints and marrow, and is a discerner of the thoughts and intents of the heart.

KJV

We should take this to mean that we need to attack this problem with the word of God itself, keeping in mind the entire time, **the will of God.**

So, now we have the necessary training, the proper equipment and the proper perspective on the type of battle and our right to fight in the battle. The next step is to get the accurate information on the goals to overcome the enemy.

The Briefing

Before any large scale military or law enforcement operation there is a briefing to give out the information necessary to carry out and achieve the goals of the mission. We need to remember one of the key reasons for destruction is a lack of knowing what the problem is and what to do about it. Again remember what is stated in Hosea 4:6

6 My people are destroyed (or also translated "cut off") for lack of knowledge: because thou hast rejected knowledge, I will also reject thee, that thou shalt be

no priest to : seeing thou hast forgotten the law of thy God, I will also forget thy children.

The key here is that destruction comes from a lack of knowledge. Isaiah 5 states it this way;

Isaiah 5:13-14

13   Therefore my people are gone into captivity, **because they have no knowledge**: and their honourable men are famished, and their multitude dried up with thirst.
14   **Therefore hell hath enlarged herself**, and opened her mouth without measure: and their glory, and their multitude, and their pomp, and he that rejoiceth, shall descend into it.
KJV

This passage of scripture says that **hell** has been enlarged due to a direct lack of knowledge. Are you beginning to see what the Word says?

This is the same way with addictions. People have not understood the spiritual root of the problem.

Okay, we have covered the root of the problem and the knowledge about it, the way to prepare, the equipment needed, there is only one thing left to do. Wage war on the spirit of addiction.

The Attack

The Final thing that we need to know is, how do we combat this fear based spirit of Addiction? There are two main keys, Faith in the Word of God and Intercessory Prayer. We have covered many key points abut the Word but we will come back, lets again talk about Intercessory Prayer.

The family of God is not based on selfishness; it is based on the love of God. If our motivations are not based on the love of God for the people we are interceding for, we need to back up and reexamine ourselves.

We need to have faith in what God said in His Word. First, we need to look at God's Word this way. If you were speaking about a subject which was the truth, let us say for example; that the sky is blue. You then told this to a person that was blind. Then the blind person did not believe you, he or she would essentially be calling you a liar. But, if this person has faith in your word, he or she would have no problem in telling other people that the sky is blue. Even if others wanted to argue about it with them, they would remain steadfast in what you have told them. The level of faith that that person had in your word is the level of faith he or she would argue your information relayed to them. We need to take God's word at face value. We can theologically argue about God's word with opinions and religious rhetoric or we can be as children and receive the word for which it is. **THE TRUTH**.

Matthew 18: 3-4 states;

3   And said, (Jesus) Verily I say unto you, Except ye be converted, and become as little children, ye shall not enter into the kingdom of heaven.
4   Whosoever therefore shall humble himself as this little child, the same is greatest in the kingdom of heaven. KJV

Have you ever tried to argue with a small child about something their parent or person they look up to has told them. No matter how hard you argue or try to convince them, you are not changing their mind. This is an example of how we need to be concerning what the word says.

Once that we have attacked with the word of God and set our faith together united to achieve victory, we need to do one more thing.

Believe

Matthew 21:22 states; and all things, whatsoever ye shall ask in prayer, believing, ye shall receive.
KJV

Mark 11:24 states; Therefore I say unto you, What things so ever ye desire, when ye pray, believe that ye receive them and ye shall have them.
KJV

Luke 11:9-10 states; 9 And I say unto you, Ask, and it shall be given you; seek, and ye shall find; knock, and it shall be opened unto you. 10 For every one that asketh receiveth; and he that seeketh findeth; and to him that knocketh it shall be opened.
KJV

John 14:13-14 states; 13 And whatsoever ye shall ask in my name, that will I do, that the Father may be glorified in the Son. 14 If ye shall ask any thing in my name, I will do it.
KJV

We must get to the point that if something does not line up with what God's Word says, then we *must* discard it because if we begin to question or doubt, victory is in jeopardy.

I know that we have covered some of the same scriptures two or three times, but we are now putting the pieces together to achieve results. Seeing how one builds upon the other while bringing the entire picture into sight. But we are not finished yet. Let us continue.

11

Standing on God's Word

What we need to understand is what the word states about what we can accomplish with God's anointing.

Matt 17:20

20 And Jesus said unto them, Because of your unbelief: for verily I say unto you, *If ye have faith* as a grain of mustard seed, ye shall say unto this mountain, Remove hence to yonder place; and it shall remove; and *nothing shall be impossible unto you.*
KJV

Matt 19:26

26 But Jesus beheld them, and said unto them, With men this is impossible; but *with God all things are possible.*
KJV

Mark 10:27

27 And Jesus looking upon them saith, With *men it is impossible*, but not with God: for *with God all things are possible.*
KJV

Luke 1:37

37 For with God *nothing shall be impossible*.
KJV

Luke 18:27

27 And he said, The things which *are impossible with men are possible with God.*
KJV

Mark 9:23

23 Jesus said unto him, If thou canst believe, *all things are possible to him that believeth.*
KJV

Mark 14:36

36 And he said, Abba, Father, *all things are possible unto thee*; take away this cup from me: nevertheless not what I will, but what thou wilt.
KJV

Phil 4:13

13 I can do *all things through Christ* which strengtheneth me.
KJV

How do we build our faith in God's Word? You might be asking yourself right now. Well, that is found in the book of Romans;

Rom 10:13-17

13 For whosoever shall call upon the name of the Lord shall be saved.
14 How then shall they call on him in whom they have not believed? and how shall they believe in him of whom they have not heard? and how shall they hear without a preacher?
15 And how shall they preach, except they be sent? as it is written, How beautiful are the feet of them that preach the gospel of peace, and bring glad tidings of good things!

16 But they have not all obeyed the gospel. For Esaias saith, Lord, who hath believed our report?

17 ***So then faith cometh by hearing***, and ***hearing*** by ***the word of God***.
KJV

You see here that we can only build our faith in God, by listening and studying God's Word. That is just plain common sense. Unfortunately, many people believe that by going through horrible trials, sickness and whatever else they can think of teaches you faith. According to the Bible, you can learn patience during those times but, Romans 10:17 is the only passage of scripture which tells you how to build faith and trust in God's Word.

12

Capturing the Vision

If we focus on what we have read so far, praying for our loved ones with intercessory prayer, believing, waiting on the Lord, standing in faith, knowing that God's Word remains true; then we are on our way to seeing results. Next, I want to talk about capturing the vision, the vision of the person we are praying for "coming to themselves", as the Prodical Son did, repenting and turning to God, accepting Jesus as their Savior and on their way to breaking the spirit of addiction. When we obtain a vision, we are looking through our eyes of faith. Look at what Proverbs says;

Proverbs 29:18

18 Where there is no *vision*, the people perish: but he that keepeth the law, happy is he
KJV

When the Prophet Habakkuk was looking for advice about certain things, look how God answered to him.

Habakkuk 2:1-3

1 I will stand upon my watch, and set me upon the tower, and will watch to see what he will say unto me, and what I shall answer when I am reproved.

2 And the LORD answered me, and said, **Write the vision**, and make it plain upon tables, that he may run that readeth it.

3 For the **vision** is yet for an appointed time, but at the end **it shall speak**, and not lie: though it tarry, wait for it; because **it will surely come**, it will not tarry.

KJV

As I was preparing the initial notes the God inspired me to write, one of the things that needed addressing was this very account of scripture. I encourage each and every one of you to take your Bible and in the front of it, write down your vision. Write the date, time, the persons name and every detail that God inspires you to write. Then when you are praying for this person, open up your Bible and look at that vision. God's word says that it will surely come, **believe the Word, not man's opinion.**

According to the Bible, one of the greatest examples of faith comes from Abraham, in the book of Romans;

Rom 4:16-21

16 Therefore it is of **faith**, that it might be by grace; to the end the promise might be sure to all the seed; not to that only which is of the law, but to that also which is of the faith of Abraham; who is the father of us all,

17 (As it is written, I have made thee a father of many nations,) before him whom **he believed**, even God, who quickeneth the dead, and **calleth those things which be not as though they were.**

18 **Who against hope believed in hope**, that he might become the father of many nations; according to that which was spoken, So shall thy seed be.

19 And being not weak in faith, he considered not his own body now dead, when he was about an hundred years old, neither yet the deadness of Sara's womb:

20 **He staggered not at the promise of God** through unbelief; but was **strong in faith, giving glory to God;**

21 **And being fully persuaded that, what he had promised, he was able also to perform.**

KJV

Abraham did not look at the situation, he looked at what God had said to him and he simply believed it.

Then he did something else, he gave glory to God in advance. He knew that things were going to change; all he had to do was wait. If you were to go to the book of Genesis and research the time period that Abraham had to wait upon the Lord, you would find it to be about twenty five years from the time that God made the first promise until Sarah conceived. As in the account of Abraham, we must do the same thing. After you capture that vision, you must simply believe, no matter what the situation looks like, because most of the time it will get worse before it gets better. But do not let go of the vision and remember what God's word says. Then after you have captured your vision, go sit down somewhere, put in your favorite Christian music in the music player and begin to praise and worship God for the breakthrough in advance. You will see it come in time. Remember that a vision is *not seeing something as it is,* it is *seeing something as it will be. BELIEVE.*

One more thing before we leave this chapter, Abraham called things that were not as though they were. We must believe when we pray, that God hears our prayer, we must remain steadfast in our faith, believing God's Word and then we must *confess*, speaking out God's promises that your friend or loved one will be delivered from the bondage of drug addiction, ignoring any circumstances that are contrary to God's Holy Word. Confessing this with your mouth is important and when people around you begin to speak negatively about the situation and are ready to give up, do not be a part of it. Remember Abraham and his situation, and "call things that be not as though they were"; and *they will begin to be.*

13

Protection until they are delivered

When God started dealing with me about believing for our family and friends to be delivered, he showed me that as we stand for their deliverance, we need to be praying and standing for their protection until they make it. Again, we are basing everything on the Word. Remember one of our initial thoughts, that it is not God's will that any should perish. Well, with that in mind, would it be safe to say that it is in God's Will that we should stand, believing God for their protection. I am confident of it. You see as we turn up the heat on Satan to leave our people alone, he is going to dig in his toe nails to try to stay in control of that situation. But you and I know that he has to leave because the Word says so. The book of James says this;

James 4:7

7   Submit yourselves therefore to God. Resist the devil, and he will flee from you. KJV

When we go on the attack of addiction, we should have already submitted ourselves to God. Then we are going to resist the devil on someone else's behalf. We must stand for as long as it takes, resisting the devil and his angels until he flees from our friends and family.

But where do we start at for protection. Let's look at the book of Isaiah for starters.

Isaiah 54:17-55:1

17 *No* weapon that is formed against thee shall prosper; and every tongue that shall rise against thee in judgment thou shalt condemn. This is the heritage of the servants of the LORD, *and their righteousness is of me, saith the LORD.*
KJV

The Word just does not get any better than that when it comes to protection. I stand on this particular scripture daily. It is powerful and makes me get goose bumps and teary-eyed every time I read it. But now let us look at Psalm 91 for an understanding of protection;

Psalms 91

1 He that dwelleth in the secret place of the most High shall abide under the shadow of the Almighty.
2 I will say of the LORD, *He is my refuge and my fortress: my God; in him will I trust.*
3 Surely he *shall deliver thee* from the snare of the fowler, and from the noisome pestilence.
4 He *shall cover thee* with his feathers, and under his wings shalt thou trust: his truth shall be thy shield and buckler.
5 Thou *shalt not be afraid* for the terror by night; nor for the arrow that flieth by day;
6 Nor for the pestilence that walketh in darkness; nor for the destruction that wasteth at noonday.
7 A thousand shall fall at thy side, and ten thousand at thy right hand; *but it shall not come nigh thee.*
8 Only with thine eyes shalt thou behold and see the reward of the wicked.
9 Because thou hast made the LORD, which is my refuge, even the most High, thy habitation;
10 There *shall no evil befall thee, neither shall any plague come nigh thy dwelling.*
11 For he *shall give his angels charge over thee*, to *keep thee in all thy ways.*
12 They shall bear thee up in their hands, lest thou dash thy foot against a stone.
13 Thou shalt tread upon the lion and adder: the young lion and the dragon shalt thou trample under feet.
14 Because he hath set his love upon me, *therefore will I deliver him: I will set him on high, because he hath known my name.*
15 *He shall call upon me, and I will answer him: I will be with him in trouble; I will deliver him*, and honour him.
16 With *long life will I satisfy him*, and shew him my salvation.
KJV

Psalms 91 can be an eye opener if you will just believe God's Word on what he has to offer. Let us elaborate a little bit on verses 11 and 12. God's word tells us that he will give his angels charge over us, to protect us. I have always found that very interesting. It must be from these scriptures, where we get the idea of a guardian angel. I hope you can see what is written in the Bible to show you that God has protected can protect and will protect if we will believe His Word. His Word (not my word or opinion) says it, I just believe it.

14

Warning, The Unbelieving Are Coming

It is time for me to forewarn you that there will be people, some that are even Christians that do not believe the Word that we have talked about. Religious tradition will not let them expand their mind and spirit to the point that they can open their hearts and just take God's Word at face value. They are afraid to take a chance. They may even say that they have tried to do that or know someone that has tried to believe God's Word on things. This is not something that you try to do. You open your heart, mind and spirit, to see that everything that God said he would do, he will still do it. You just believe it, leaving all doubt and unbelief behind.

Do you want to know what unbelief is? Let us look at what God's Word says about unbelief in Hebrews;

Heb 3:12-4:1

12 Take heed, brethren, *lest there be in any of you an evil heart of unbelief*, in departing from the living God.
13 But exhort one another daily, while it is called To day; lest any of you be hardened through the deceitfulness of sin.
14 For we are made partakers of Christ, if we hold the beginning of our confidence stedfast unto the end;
15 *While it is said, To day if ye will hear his voice, harden not your hearts, as in the provocation.*

16 *For some, when they had heard, did provoke: howbeit not all that came out of Egypt by Moses.*

17 *But with whom was he grieved forty years?* was it not with them that had sinned, whose carcases fell in the wilderness?

18 And to whom sware he that they should not enter into his rest, but to them that believed not?

19 *So we see that they could not enter in because of unbelief.*

KJV

In verse 12 the Bible relates unbelief to having an evil heart. Then this passage of scripture tells why the children of Israel had such a hard time and why many of them could not enter into their own promised land. Look again at verse 19, it was because of their unbelief. But let's not stop there let us take a further look in Mark.

Mark 16:14

14 Afterward he appeared unto the eleven as they sat at meat, and *upbraided them with their unbelief and hardness of heart*, because they believed not them which had seen him after he was risen.

KJV

Here, again we find that unbelief is a heart issue. But let us look a little further at this issue. This time we will look in the book of Matthew.

Matt 13:57-58

57 And *they were offended in him*. But Jesus said unto them, A prophet is not without honour, save in his own country, and in his own house.

58 And *he did not many mighty works there because of their unbelief.*

KJV

Can you imagine anyone that would get offended at Jesus? Well, when you start telling people that you believe for so-and-so to be delivered from the bondage of drug addiction, do not be surprised if someone gets offended. Next, we find out that the same unbelief limited Jesus' ability to heal people. Let us look at Mark 6 for a better understanding;

Mark 6:5

5 And he *could there do no mighty work*, save that he laid his hands upon a few sick folk, and healed them.

KJV

Here is the question that I want you to ask yourself, and I want you to ask others when they come at you with unbelief of God's Word. Do you, deep down inside your inner-being want to believe that God can do all things and that we can do all things through Christ? Let us take one look at Philippians 4:13,

Phil 4:13

13 I can do all things through Christ which strengtheneth me.
KJV

Do not just answer the question; take a few minutes to really let that question settle into your spirit. I am sure that the answer is yes, I do want to believe. Then if that is the case, remember, the key to faith is believing as children, just open your heart to God's Word and let it pour in.

Folks, the only person that prays for your friend or loved one may be you. It is time to take back our families and friends from the grips of Satan and the bondage of drug addiction. You can see why it is so important for you to not listen to outside sources and doubt God's Word. *You* may be the difference between life and death for this person. ***BELIEVE!***

15

In Closing

In closing, I would like to thank you for reading this book. I hope that the Word inside of it has given you a new outlook on life. I truly believe that if you will do what is outlined in this book, you will see results. You have to because God's Word says so, and according to the book of Isaiah;

Isaiah 55:11

11 So shall my word be that goeth forth out of my mouth: ***it shall not return unto me void***, but it ***shall accomplish*** that which I please, ***and it shall prosper*** in the thing whereto I sent it.
KJV

Remember the steps

1. Understand the Will of God.
2. Understand and get into Intercessory Prayer for the person you want to see delivered.
3. Unite in prayer with others believing for the deliverance.
4. Keep your Faith Steadfast.
5. Stay in God's Love.
6. Pray for Wisdom and Understanding.
7. Get into your spiritual combat readiness.

8. Capture your vision.
9. Confess your vision daily, "calling things that be not as though they were".
10. Pray and believe for their protection
11. When you have done all . . . . **STAND**

Finally, remember what the Word says about believing in Mark 9:23 "If thou canst believe, **all things** are possible to him that believeth". KJV

This is the key that will separate you from the rest of the world.

Prayer of Agreement

Dear Heavenly Father, as I come before you today, I stand with the reader of this book, believing that your word is true. Your word says that if we have the faith the size of a mustard seed, we can say mountain, be removed and cast into the sea and expect it to happen. Today I stand with this person, saying to the mountain, that is drug addiction in the life of one of your creations, be removed from this person. Father, I believe that this spirit of addiction will be lifted from them, just as the prodigal son came to himself; I fully expect that this person will come to himself and repent of their sins, turning their life over to you. Believing that you will come into their lives, replacing that spirit of addiction with one of power and of love and of a sound mind. I stand in unity with the reader of this book, capturing the vision of drug addiction being lifted from all their friends and loved ones. Each and every reader that will take a stand for you and your word will see that you are a good and just God, who sent His own Son, Jesus, here to this earth so that we could be brought back into right standing with you. I also stand with the reader of this book, believing for your protection over the person in bondage, believing that you will give your angels charge over them and that you would encamp your angels round about them, confessing and believing your word, that no weapon formed against them will prosper. I truly thank you dear Lord for the reader of this book, and it is my prayer for them that you would bless all their endeavors and lead them as they stand for others. I give you dear Father all the praise, honor and glory, in Jesus' name we pray,
Amen

Reference Study Scriptures

Job 36:11-12

11 If they obey and serve him, they shall spend their days in prosperity, and their years in pleasures.
12 But if they obey not, they shall perish by the sword, and they shall die without knowledge.
KJV

Psalms 30:1-5

30:1 A Psalm and Song at the dedication of the house of David.
    I will extol thee, O LORD; for thou hast lifted me up, and hast not made my foes to rejoice over me.
2   O LORD my God, I cried unto thee, and thou hast healed me.
3   O LORD, thou hast brought up my soul from the grave: thou hast kept me alive, that I should not go down to the pit.
4   Sing unto the LORD, O ye saints of his, and give thanks at the remembrance of his holiness.
5   For his anger endureth but a moment; in his favour is life: weeping may endure for a night, but joy cometh in the morning.
KJV

Psalms 103

Bless the LORD, O my soul: and all that is within me, bless his holy name.

2　Bless the LORD, O my soul, and forget not all his benefits:
3　Who forgiveth all thine iniquities; who healeth all thy diseases;
4　Who redeemeth thy life from destruction; who crowneth thee with lovingkindness and tender mercies;
5　Who satisfieth thy mouth with good things; so that thy youth is renewed like the eagle's.
6　The LORD executeth righteousness and judgment for all that are oppressed.
7　He made known his ways unto Moses, his acts unto the children of Israel.
8　The LORD is merciful and gracious, slow to anger, and plenteous in mercy.
9　He will not always chide: neither will he keep his anger for ever.
10　He hath not dealt with us after our sins; nor rewarded us according to our iniquities.
11　For as the heaven is high above the earth, so great is his mercy toward them that fear him.
12　As far as the east is from the west, so far hath he removed our transgressions from us.
13　Like as a father pitieth his children, so the LORD pitieth them that fear him.
14　For he knoweth our frame; he remembereth that we are dust.
15　As for man, his days are as grass: as a flower of the field, so he flourisheth.
16　For the wind passeth over it, and it is gone; and the place thereof shall know it no more.
17　But the mercy of the LORD is from everlasting to everlasting upon them that fear him, and his righteousness unto children's children;
18　To such as keep his covenant, and to those that remember his commandments to do them.
19　The LORD hath prepared his throne in the heavens; and his kingdom ruleth over all.
20　Bless the LORD, ye his angels, that excel in strength, that do his commandments, hearkening unto the voice of his word.
21　Bless ye the LORD, all ye his hosts; ye ministers of his, that do his pleasure.
22　Bless the LORD, all his works in all places of his dominion: bless the LORD, O my soul.
KJV

Matthew 5:44

44　But I say unto you, Love your enemies, bless them that curse you, do good to them that hate you, and pray for them which despitefully use you, and persecute you;
KJV

Ezekiel 33:11

11 Say unto them, As I live, saith the Lord GOD, I have no pleasure in the death of the wicked; but that the wicked turn from his way and live: turn ye, turn ye from your evil ways; for why will ye die, O house of Israel?
KJV

John 5:36-40

36 But I have greater witness than that of John: for the works which the Father hath given me to finish, the same works that I do, bear witness of me, that the Father hath sent me.
37 And the Father himself, which hath sent me, hath borne witness of me. Ye have neither heard his voice at any time, nor seen his shape.
38 And ye have not his word abiding in you: for whom he hath sent, him ye believe not.
39 Search the scriptures; for in them ye think ye have eternal life: and they are they which testify of me.
40 And ye will not come to me, that ye might have life.
KJV

Hebrews 4:12

12 For the word of God is quick, and powerful, and sharper than any twoedged sword, piercing even to the dividing asunder of soul and spirit, and of the joints and marrow, and is a discerner of the thoughts and intents of the heart.
KJV

James 1:1-8

1 James, a servant of God and of the Lord Jesus Christ, to the twelve tribes which are scattered abroad, greeting.
2 My brethren, count it all joy when ye fall into divers temptations;
3 Knowing this, that the trying of your faith worketh patience.
4 But let patience have her perfect work, that ye may be perfect and entire, wanting nothing.
5 If any of you lack wisdom, let him ask of God, that giveth to all men liberally, and upbraideth not; and it shall be given him.
6 But let him ask in faith, nothing wavering. For he that wavereth is like a wave of the sea driven with the wind and tossed.
7 For let not that man think that he shall receive any thing of the Lord.

8   A double minded man is unstable in all his ways.
KJV

Hebrews 2:13-15

13   And again, I will put my trust in him. And again, Behold I and the children which God hath given me.
14   Forasmuch then as the children are partakers of flesh and blood, he also himself likewise took part of the same; that through death he might destroy him that had the power of death, that is, the devil;
15   And deliver them who through fear of death were all their lifetime subject to bondage.
KJV

May God Bless you and keep you in all your endeavors.